My SPECIAL

Book for Dad!

Written by

....

© The Life Graduate Publishing Group

All Rights Reserved

No part of this book may be scanned, reproduced or distributed in any printed or electronic form without the prior permission of the author or publisher.

That's me!

About the Author

My Name is _____

I am _____ Yrs old:

My Favorite thing to do is:

_____
_____
_____
_____
_____
_____

Dear Dad,
I wrote this book
for you because......

#01

DAD,
I LOVE YOU
BECAUSE....

_____
_____
_____
_____

#02

DAD, YOU ARE FUNNY WHEN....

_____

_____

_____

_____

DAD, THIS IS MY FAVORITE PHOTO OF US

#03

Stick Photo Here!

#04

DAD,
MY FAVORITE HOLIDAY WITH YOU WAS WHEN WE ....

_____
_____
_____
_____

DAD,
THIS IS A DRAWING OF YOU AT WORK

#05

#06
THIS IS A TRACING OF MY HAND!

trace your hand here

#07

DAD,

THESE ARE 3 THINGS THAT YOU DO THAT ARE KIND..

#1 _____

#2 _____

#3 _____

#08

DAD,
YOU COOK THE BEST.......

_____
_____
_____
_____

#09
DAD, YOUR BIRTHDAY IS

DAY

MONTH

YOU ARE………YRS OLD

#10

DAD, YOU LAUGH THE LOUDEST WHEN.......

_____

_____

_____

_____

#11
DAD, THE BEST THING ABOUT YOUR JOB IS........

_____
_____
_____
_____

#12

DAD, I WANT YOU TO SHOW ME HOW TO……..

_____

_____

_____

_____

#13

**DAD,
YOUR FAVOURITE
TIME OF THE YEAR
IS........**

BECAUSE........

#14

**DAD,
YOU LOVE ME
WHEN I.......**

_____
_____
_____
_____

#15

**DAD,
YOU LOOK LIKE...**

_____

FROM THE T.V!

#16

DAD,
I THINK YOU ARE THE BEST AT.......

_____

_____

_____

_____

#17

DAD,
THIS IS A DRAWING OF YOU AND ME

DAD,
YOUR FAVORITE FOOD TO EAT IS........

#18

#19
DAD, THESE ARE THE 3 THINGS I LOVE ABOUT YOU MOST

#1 _____

#2 _____

#3 _____

DAD, YOU ARE SO KIND WHEN YOU.....

#20

#21
DAD, YOU DIDN'T KNOW THIS, BUT I LOVE TO.......

_____

_____

_____

_____

SPECIAL
MOMENTS

insert photos

SPECIAL
MOMENTS

iNSERT PHOTOS

books in the

JR. AUTHOR SERIES

 Perfect for our little authors!

www.ingramcontent.com/pod-product-compliance
Lightning Source LLC
LaVergne TN
LVHW051933070526
838200LV00077B/4638